D0471546

NEEDLEPOINT

Simple to Sew

Simple-to-Sew

NEEDLEPOINT

*Master new sewing skills with these
simple-to-make projects*

HILARY MORE

CHARTWELL
BOOKS, INC.

A QUINTET BOOK

Published by Chartwell Books
A Division of Book Sales, Inc.
114 Northfield Avenue
Edison, New Jersey 00837

This edition produced for sale in the U.S.A., its
territories and dependencies only.

Copyright © 1996 Quintet Publishing Limited.
All rights reserved. No part of this publication may be
reproduced, stored in a retrieval system or transmitted
in any form or by any means, electronic, mechanical,
photocopying, recording or otherwise, without the
permission of the copyright holder.

ISBN 0-7858-0362-9

This book was designed and produced by
Quintet Publishing Limited
6 Blundell Street
London N7 9BH

Creative Director: Richard Dewing
Designer: Isobel Gillan
Project Editor: Diana Steedman
Editor: Samantha Gray
Photographer: Andrew Sydenham
Illustrator: Terry Evans
Chart Illustrator: Jenny Dooge

Typeset in Great Britain by
Central Southern Typesetters, Eastbourne
Manufactured by Eray Scan Pte. Ltd., Singapore
Printed by Star Standard Industries (Pte.) Ltd., Singapore

ACKNOWLEDGMENTS
The Publishers are grateful to the following
for their help with this publication:
Coats Craft UK, DMC Creative World Ltd, Paterna Persian Yarn,
Readicut Wool, Framecraft, Offray Ribbon, Jane Hibbert,
Sue Davies of Brethyn Brith, Jan Eaton, Beryl Miller,
Caroline Palmer, Dawn Marie Parmley, Angela Bartlett,
and to Creativity, Needlecraft Specialists,
45 New Oxford Street, London.

CONTENTS

INTRODUCTION

Welcome to the wonderful world of needlepoint! Needlepoint is embroidery worked in a variety of different yarns over a canvas background. Often called tapestry or canvaswork, it appeals to all needleworkers because you can quickly create beautiful things for the home and family. Today this type of stitchery has broken away from its traditional past of complicated scenic designs worked in fine yarn to embrace a collection of styles and techniques using wool, embroidery floss, ribbon, and fabric, in fact almost any type of yarn which can be used over canvas.

Needlepoint is simple and fun to do, and once you have mastered a few simple stitches, you can create a host of patterns and designs. If you are a beginner, start with a simple project, such as the Country Scene picture on page 20 – it's a perfect first-time project. At the other end of the scale, the sumptuous floral tieback on page 43 will delight a more experienced stitcher.

Before you begin, read the following section on the materials and all the simple techniques you need to know. Then each of the projects comes complete with a chart, key, and step-by-step instructions to help you produce a stunning piece of needlepoint.

Happy stitching!

MATERIALS AND EQUIPMENT

Canvas

Canvas is specifically made as the base for needlepoint. It is woven from stiffened cotton or linen and is generally available in white, buff, or dark beige. Canvas is graded by the number of threads or holes to 1 inch. This is the mesh or gauge size – the smaller the number, the coarser the canvas. Choose the best quality canvas you can afford, because this will provide a firm foundation on which to build your stitches and give the needlepoint a long life.

To work out how much canvas you need for a project, add an extra 3 inches all around for standard and large pieces, and 2 inches for a small piece of work. This extra border of canvas allows for stretching and mounting. Canvas can be bought by the yard or by the piece. The two main types of canvas are plain or interlocking mono and penelope canvas.

Mono canvas is woven with single crossing threads – horizontally and vertically. The best variety is interlock canvas, in which the threads are twisted and bonded together, providing a very firm background. Mono canvas is easy to use, especially for a beginner, because any stitch can be worked over the even grid surface.

Penelope canvas has pairs of crossing threads interwoven horizontally and vertically. The double threads can be gently parted and used as a single canvas to gain smoother curved lines, and for areas of fine detailed work.

Rug canvas is a coarse interlock canvas which is available in a range of different widths.

Plastic canvas is bought in small sheets or pre-cut shapes, such as circles, and is generally used for three-dimensional pieces of canvaswork. It is easy to cut and will not fray. Plastic canvas is a good choice for children learning to stitch.

Yarns

Choose a yarn appropriate to your needlepoint project, and then match the yarn to the type and gauge of canvas. It must be thick enough to completely cover the canvas, but the threaded needle must still be able to pass through the canvas mesh without pushing the threads apart and distorting the canvas. On large-gauge canvas, several strands can be used together to cover the canvas threads. Buy all the yarn at the beginning of a project since dye lots can change and even a slight variation will show up, especially in a large area of one color. Always work a test piece, using your chosen yarn on the chosen canvas, to see how the finished piece will look.

Wool is the traditional yarn for needlepoint. Choose from tapestry, crewel, and Persian yarns. Once you are more experienced at stitching, you can try a range of different fibers for experimental work, but use wool when you first begin to get the feel of needlepoint.

Tapestry yarn is a firm, tightly twisted single 100% wool strand which cannot be divided. It is available in 11-yard skeins in a huge range of colors. Tapestry yarn can also be bought in ¾ ounce hanks (grounding wool) in a smaller range of popular background colors.

Crewel yarn is a fine two-ply yarn used for delicate canvaswork. It can be used as a single strand, or two, three, four, or more strands can be used together on thicker canvases. Each color is available in a wide range of shades, making this yarn a good choice for detailed shading and ideal for blending different colors together to create muted shades.

Persian yarn is slightly thicker than crewel yarn. A loosely twisted three-strand yarn, it can be divided or added to for working on different size canvas and to blend different colors together.

Cotton embroidery floss is made up of multiple strands of mercerized cotton, loosely twisted together. It can be used as a single strand or in groups – nine strands of floss is equal to a single strand of tapestry yarn. Separate the strands before regrouping into the number of threads needed for the project.

Matte embroidery cotton is a soft, fairly thick twisted thread with a dull finish. It is a successful alternative to tapestry yarn for canvaswork.

Metallic threads are available in an extensive range of different thicknesses and shades, and small amounts can be mixed in or used over previously stitched sections.

Needles

Tapestry needles have rounded, blunt tips which do not split the yarn or the canvas threads. Their large eyes can accommodate different threads and thicker yarns. Needles are graded into size by thickness – the higher the number, the finer the needle.

As a quick guide: use a size 18 for 10- and 12-gauge canvas; size 20 for 14-gauge canvas; size 22 for 16- and 18-gauge canvas, and size 24 for fine 22- and 24-gauge canvases.

Frames

Mount the canvas in either a square or rectangular frame; there are two basic types:

Simple stretcher frames are made from two pairs of artists' stretchers. These are lengths of wood with mitered and slotted corners, which can be quickly put together. The canvas is held on the frame with thumbtacks.

Rotating frames are the most common of the frames. They come in a variety of sizes and are composed of two horizontal rods slotted into two side pieces. Each rod has a strip of webbing tape stapled along one edge. The rollers are set into two straight side pieces and held firmly with four butterfly screws, one in each corner. These frames can be mounted on floor-standing supports, leaving both hands free for stitching.

Other Equipment Required

Scissors – use large dressmaker's scissors for cutting canvas, and a small, sharp-pointed pair for trimming and cutting yarn.

Floor-standing needlepoint frames allow both hands to be free for stitching.

Thimble – if you normally wear a thimble for sewing, you'll find it useful when stitching needlepoint to protect the middle (pushing) finger.

Masking tape – bind the raw canvas edges to protect the yarns and your hands.

Buttonhole thread, used in a sewing needle for lacing the canvas to a rotating frame and for holding the finished canvas over a backing board, ready for framing.

Daylight bulb – fit this special type of light bulb in a side lamp to help you see the exact yarn colors during dark or gloomy days.

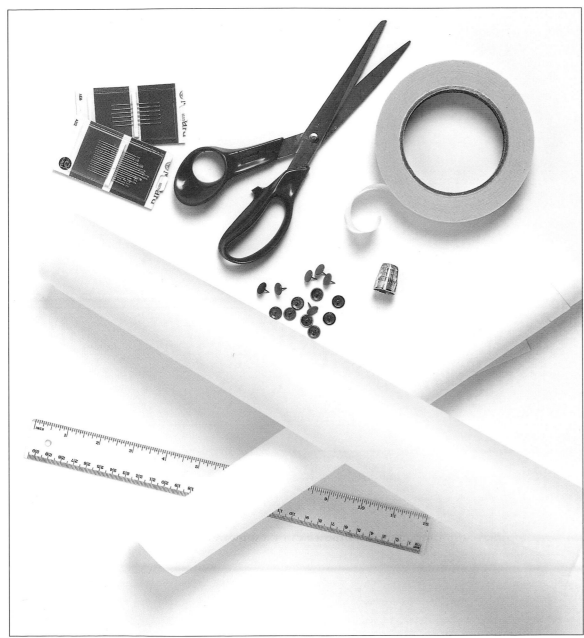

Tracing and graph paper are needed for designing and transferring designs. A thick, black, waterproof felt-tip pen, ruler, and T-square are also useful for marking the canvas before stitching.

Firm board and thumbtacks – when the finished piece of needlepoint is complete, pin the canvas over blotting or tissue paper to block the canvas back into shape.

TECHNIQUES

You don't need any special skills to work a piece of needlepoint. Once you have learned a couple of basic stitches, you can create a masterpiece! Just use the following techniques as a guide to help you gain the best results:

Preparing the canvas

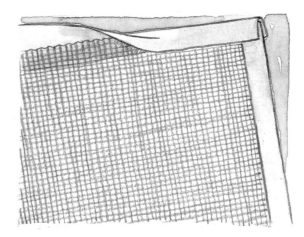

Cut canvas alongside a thread in both directions. To protect your hands and clothes from catching on the raw canvas, and to prevent the edges from unraveling, cover with masking tape. Cut a length of 1in wide tape for each side, and simply fold evenly in half over the canvas edges. Press the masking tape firmly in position.

Working in a frame

Unless you are working with plastic canvas or on a very small piece of canvas, it is advisable to stitch your canvas in a needlepoint frame. It is a matter of preference, but if you learn to use a

frame from the beginning, you will find it easier to work – both hands will be free – and you will gain an even result. A needlepoint frame keeps the canvas stretched taut, making it easier to stitch in two movements – the correct way to work a piece of needlepoint – up through the canvas and back down again. With more experience, you will find that you can stitch with a flowing rhythm, maintain an even tension, and effect the minimum distortion to the canvas.

Fitting the canvas into a frame

1 Cut the canvas to the correct size for the project, at least 3 inches larger all around on standard and large projects, and 2 inches larger all around on smaller pieces. Bind all edges with masking tape, as shown.

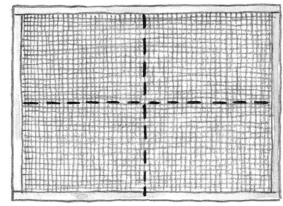

2 Use a doubled length of contrasting sewing thread to baste across the canvas both lengthwise and widthwise to mark the center of the canvas. Alternatively, use a permanent ink felt tip-pen to mark the center of the canvas on each side. Use a pencil to mark the center of the webbing tapes.

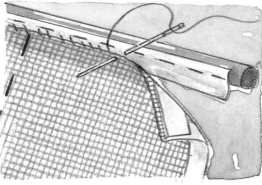

3 Turn under approximately ⅜ inch of canvas and, matching center marks, oversew the canvas to the tape along one rod. Repeat, to stitch the opposite edge of canvas to the row of webbing tape on the opposite rod. Begin stitching in the center and work outward to the edge on either side.

4 Assemble the frame. Wind any excess canvas around one of the rods, and tighten the screws to hold the canvas firm and taut.

5 To help support the side edges of the canvas, use buttonhole thread or fine string to lace the side edges of the canvas around the side sections of the frame.

Working from a chart

A needlepoint chart is made up of a grid of squares, with each square representing one stitch or one hole of canvas. Charts are not actual-size. In the materials list at the beginning of a project, you'll find the canvas gauge size stated – buy this size of canvas to achieve the finished size of the project. To enlarge or reduce the size of the project, simply work over a finer canvas or over a canvas with a larger gauge count.

1 Mark the center lines of the canvas – these will match up with the center lines marked on the chart. To make it even easier to follow the chart, you can subdivide the canvas into ten square sections to match up with the heavier guide lines found on most charts. Count out the squares, and mark across the canvas as before.
2 Each symbol or color on a chart represents the color and stitch with which that area is worked. Follow the key that goes with the chart, and match the symbol or color to the yarn color, then work the number of stitches shown on the chart. Use the marked lines as a guide, removing them as soon as you have stitched over them.

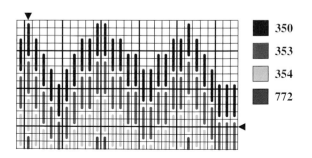

■	350
■	353
▨	354
■	772

Working from an actual-size design

Instead of using a chart, actual-size needlepoint designs can be marked on the canvas with a permanent ink felt-tip pen, or painted onto the canvas using waterproof paints. Mark out the outline before fitting the canvas into a needlepoint frame.

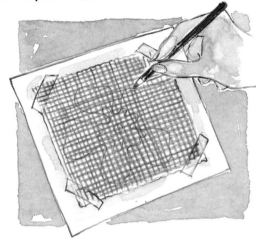

1 If necessary, enlarge the design on a photocopier to the desired finished size. Go over the outline with a black felt-tip pen, so you have a strong, clear outline. Mark the center of the design on each side.
2 Tape the design flat on a board. Matching center marks, tape the canvas over the design. You will see the design through the canvas threads. Mark the outline onto the canvas, following the outline of the design. Make sure that the outline goes around the canvas holes to make it easier to follow when stitching.
3 Alternatively, use waterproof paints to paint the design onto the canvas in your chosen colors. Then you can match the areas to the yarns when stitching.

Beginning to stitch

1 Cut approximately 18 inches of yarn. If the yarn is too long, the continuous rubbing against the canvas threads will make it fray and wear thin. Thread one end through a tapestry needle, wrapping the yarn tightly around the needle eye. Slide the yarn off the needle and thread through the eye. Knot the opposite end.
2 Take the threaded needle through the canvas, from the right side to the wrong side, leaving the knot ¾ inch in front of where the stitching will begin.

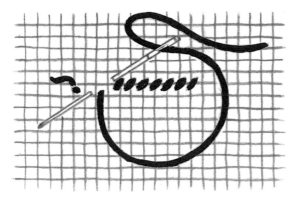

3 Bring the needle back to the right side of the canvas at the position for the first stitch. Work the first few stitches over the canvas and yarn end. When the knot is reached, cut it off and continue stitching.

4 Start new lengths of yarn by sliding the needle under the backs of a few worked stitches on the wrong side of the canvas, then bringing it through the correct hole to the right side, ready for stitching.

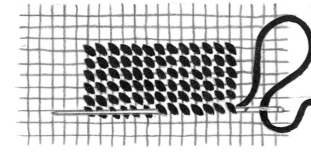

5 To end a length of yarn, slide the needle under a few stitches at the back of the canvas. Trim off the end close to the canvas.

6 Try to avoid beginning and ending yarn in the same place, row after row, because a ridge will form on the right side of the canvas.

Hints and tips for successful stitching

- Work each stitch in two movements, with the left hand on top of the canvas and the right hand underneath. Feed the needle up through the canvas to the right side and back down to the wrong side. You can only work this two-step method when the canvas is stretched taut in a needlepoint frame. With practice, you will gain a flowing rhythm of stitching and maintain an even stitch tension with the minimum of canvas distortion.

- It is important to keep an even tension when stitching. Before you work any new stitch, practice on a spare piece of canvas to gauge the tension. If the stitches are too loose, they will not cover the canvas. If the stitches are too tight, the canvas will pucker and stretch out of shape.

- Try to come up through an empty hole of canvas and go down through the canvas in a partially filled hole. This will help to smooth down the yarn.

- The yarn will become twisted as you stitch – simply let the needle drop and the yarn will naturally untwist itself.

- Move the needle along the yarn as you stitch, to prevent the yarn from wearing thin where it is threaded through the needle eye.

- When stitching a tiny piece of canvas that can not fit into a needlepoint frame, place the canvas centrally on a spare piece of fabric and baste firmly together. Set the fabric in an embroidery hoop. Separate the rings; place the fabric over the smaller ring. Fit the larger ring over the top; press in place and tighten. Turn over and cut away the fabric from behind the canvas area – you can then stitch the canvas in the usual way.

Correcting mistakes

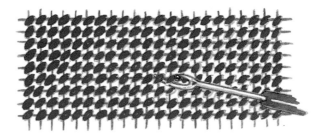

1 If you make a mistake, stitches can be quickly unpicked. Use a pair of small, sharply pointed scissors to snip through one stitch, then, using the blunt end of a tapestry needle, gently ease out the offending stitches. If you have a row of stitches to remove, use a seam ripper. Slide it just under the stitches on the wrong side to cut them. Re-stitch using a new length of yarn.

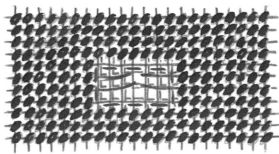

2 If you accidentally snip a canvas thread, a new piece of canvas can be grafted over the hole. Unpick the stitches surrounding the hole over a 1½ inch area. Cut a 1½ inch square of canvas with the same gauge count. Position the canvas square over the hole on the wrong side of the main canvas, match the canvas threads, and baste in place. Now stitch over the area again in the usual way, working through both layers of canvas.

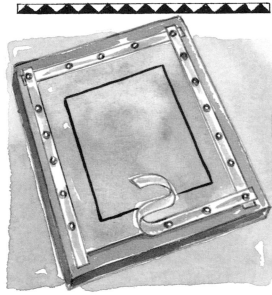

Blocking a piece of needlepoint

When you have finished a piece of needlepoint, you may find it has been pulled out of shape. Generally this can be cured by a steam-press on the wrong side, while gently pulling the canvas back into shape. However, if the canvas is badly distorted, the best method is to stretch and block it back into shape.

1 Mark out the finished outline on a clean sheet of blotting or tissue paper, and pin this over a clean, flat wooden board.

2 Dampen the back of the needlepoint using a wet sponge or plant mister. The water is used just to soften the canvas, so do not over-wet the canvas.

3 Lay the canvas, right side up, over the board. Gently pull the canvas to match the outline of the needlepoint to the marked outline on the paper. Pin in place with thumbtacks. Begin pinning at the center top and work outward, straighten the base edge to match, and, finally, stretch and pin the sides in the same way. Use a T-square to help check any right-angle corners. Space the thumbtacks approximately 1 inch apart.

4 Check that the canvas is straight, and leave to dry thoroughly for approximately 24 hours.

WELCOME TO SPRING

Finished size: 6 x 5 inches

This tiny springtime picture, complete with *gamboling lambs, is worked entirely in half-cross stitch using soft embroidery cotton over a 14-gauge canvas, so it's a good project for a beginner.*

YOU WILL NEED

- 12 x 10 inch piece of white interlock mono canvas with 14 holes to 1 inch
- masking tape
- Anchor matte embroidery cotton in the following colors and amounts: two skeins of off-white 2, one skein each of geranium 11, cornflower 147, grass green 242, almond green 260, dark almond green 262, canary yellow 288, black 403, beige 679, dusty pink 892, and kingfisher 9159
- tapestry needle, size 20
- basting thread in contrasting color
- needlepoint frame
- picture frame and mount board

1 **To work** To prevent the canvas edges from unraveling, and to protect your hands and clothes, fold masking tape evenly in half over the raw canvas edges.

2 Using contrasting thread, baste across the canvas both lengthwise and widthwise to mark the center (see Techniques, page 10).

3 Mount the canvas into the frame (see Techniques, page 10).

4 The chart shows the complete design for the picture. The center is marked with black arrowheads – match these up with the lines of basting stitches on the canvas. Each square on the chart represents one half-cross stitch, worked over one canvas thread intersection.

5 Beginning in the center, work the whole design in half-cross stitch, following the chart and key.

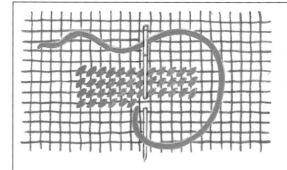

Half-cross stitch. Bring the needle out of the canvas and take a small diagonal stitch over one canvas thread intersection with the needle vertical, bringing it out of the canvas directly below. On the wrong side of the canvas the stitches will be vertical. Make sure that all the stitches slant in the same direction.

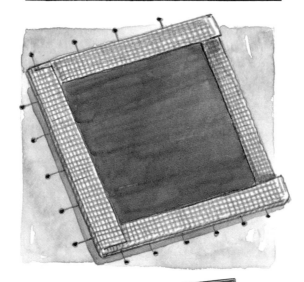

6 **To finish** When the needlepoint is complete, remove it from the frame. Peel off the masking tape from the canvas edges. Press the needlepoint on the wrong side over a damp cloth, gently pulling the canvas back into shape (see Techniques, page 13).

7 Remove the backing board from the frame and place the needlepoint centrally over it. Attach the needlepoint to the top edge of the board with a line of tacks. Pull the canvas over the bottom edge of the board and hold in place with tacks in the same way. Repeat on both sides.

8 Keep checking that the design is central and that the canvas is taut. Turn the board over to the wrong side and, using a doubled sewing thread, lace the two edges together from side to side and from top to bottom.

9 Remove the tacks and replace the board inside the frame. Add another piece of cardboard, and tape across frame back to secure.

DECORATIVE ADDRESS BOOK

Finished size: to fit an address book 6⅛ x 4⅛ inches

This address book, with its delightful needlepoint cover, will inspire you to keep an up-to-date record of the addresses of your family and friends. Embroidered in tapestry yarn over a 14-gauge canvas, the whole design is worked in traditional tent stitch.

YOU WILL NEED

- masking tape
- 16¼ x 12¼ inch piece of white mono canvas with 14 holes to 1 inch
- black, fine-point felt-tip pen with permanent ink
- basting thread in contrasting color
- needlepoint frame
- DMC tapestry yarn in the following colors and amounts: 10 skeins of blue 7820, one skein each of orange 7947, purple 7708, red 7666, turquoise 7996, yellow 7973, and green 7911
- tapestry needle, size 20
- address book with a front face 4⅛ x 6⅛ inches and ½ inch thick spine
- 1 yard of ⅝ inch wide blue binding tape
- sewing thread to match binding

1 To work To protect your hands and clothes, and the yarn from catching on the canvas, fold masking tape evenly in half over the raw canvas edges.

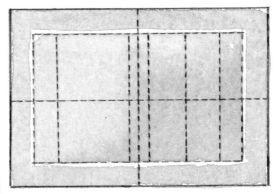

2 Following the diagram and using the measurements of the address book, mark the outline of the cover centrally on the canvas with the felt-tip pen. Mark ¾ inch deep pockets on either end of the cover. With a line of basting stitches worked in a contrasting color thread, mark the center of the front cover section.

3 The chart shows the complete design for the front cover. The center of the design is marked by arrowheads – match these up with the marked lines on the canvas. Each square on the chart represents one tent stitch worked over one canvas thread intersection.

4 Mount the canvas into the frame (see Techniques, page 10).

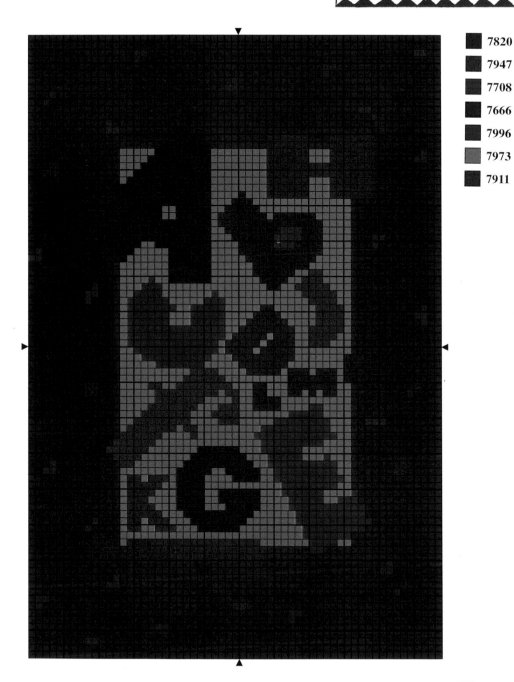

■	7820
■	7947
■	7708
■	7666
■	7996
■	7973
■	7911

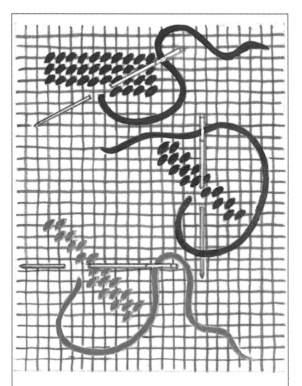

Tent stitch. To work horizontal rows, bring the needle out of the canvas and take a small diagonal stitch over one canvas thread intersection. Take the needle down diagonally behind one horizontal and two vertical threads, then bring it out ready for the next stitch. On the wrong side, the stitches will be slightly longer diagonal stitches.

To work diagonally down the canvas, take the needle diagonally up over one canvas thread intersection then pass it vertically down behind two horizontal canvas threads.

To work diagonally up the canvas, the needle is passed horizontally behind two vertical canvas threads.

5 The design is worked in tent stitch throughout. Stitch the front cover following the chart and key. Then work the spine and back cover section in blue 7820, with odd stitches worked in turquoise 7996 and purple 7708 scattered around, in a similar way to the background of the front cover.

6 **To finish** Remove the completed needlepoint from the frame. Peel off the masking tape from the canvas edges. Press the needlepoint on the wrong side over a damp cloth, gently pulling the canvas back into shape.

7 Trim the canvas to within ⅜ inch of the needlepoint. Pin and stitch the binding along the edges of the needlepoint all around the cover. Miter each corner, and join binding edges together to fit.

8 Turn the binding at top and bottom edges to the inside and press well. Catchstitch the edge of the binding down.

9 Turn in ⅜ inch of needlepoint at each side to form pockets; press well. Catchstitch the pocket edges to the top and bottom of the cover to secure the pockets.

10 Insert the address book by slipping the cover ends inside the cover.

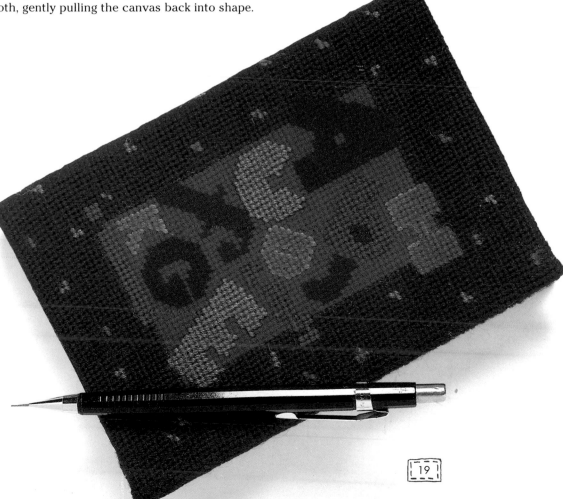

A COUNTRY SCENE

Finished size: approximately 7 x 6½ inches

Quick to stitch, this charming country scene is worked in long stitch over a 14-gauge canvas. When the needlepoint stitches are completed, straight stitch, backstitch, and French knots are added to bring character to this little picture.

YOU WILL NEED

- 11 x 10 inch piece of mono canvas with 14 holes to 1 inch
- masking tape
- Anchor Tapisserie yarn in the following shades: one skein each of white 8000, china blue 8624, laurel 9006, cornflower blue 8688, cathedral blue 8792, pale cornflower blue 8682, beige brown 9636, jade 8966, emerald 8988, spring green 9114, paprika 8240, and yellow/orange 8116
- Anchor embroidery floss: one skein of black 403
- tapestry needle, size 20
- crewel needle for embroidery details
- needlepoint frame
- picture frame and mount board

1 **To work** To protect your hands and clothes, and the yarn from catching on the canvas, fold masking tape evenly in half over the raw canvas edges.

2 The chart shows the complete picture actual-size. Trace the design and mark it on to a clean sheet of paper, going over it with black felt-tip pen. Tape the design flat, then tape the canvas centrally over the design. Use the felt-tip pen to draw the design onto the canvas (see Techniques, page 11). Remove the tape and mount the canvas into the frame.

3 Work the picture following the chart and key for colors of the tapestry yarns. The whole picture is worked in long satin stitch, working over a different number of canvas threads to completely fill each marked area.

4 When the needlepoint stitches are complete, embroider the smoke in backstitch using black embroidery floss. Work a French knot in black embroidery floss for each duck's eye, and use yellow/orange 8116 to work the flowers along the riverbank.

5 When the stitching is complete, remove the canvas from the frame. Press lightly on the wrong side over a damp cloth, gently pulling the canvas back into shape.

6 Frame the picture in the same way as for the Spring Picture (see page 16).

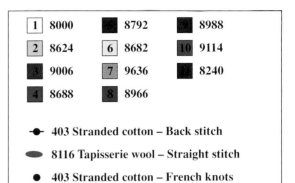

1	8000	5	8792	9	8988
2	8624	6	8682	10	9114
3	9006	7	9636		8240
4	8688	8	8966		

—●— 403 Stranded cotton – Back stitch

⬭ 8116 Tapisserie wool – Straight stitch

● 403 Stranded cotton – French knots

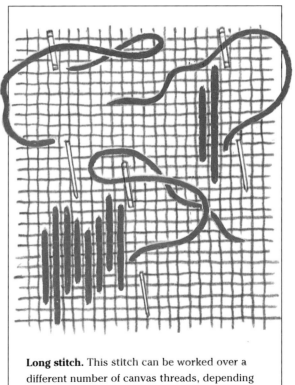

Long stitch. This stitch can be worked over a different number of canvas threads, depending on the area of the design. Always work in the same direction to keep an even tension.

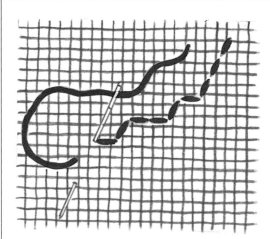

Backstitch. Bring the needle out of the canvas and take a backward stitch, bringing the needle out the same distance in front of the first stitch. Then go into the first hole, and out a stitch length in front. Keep repeating the same stitch.

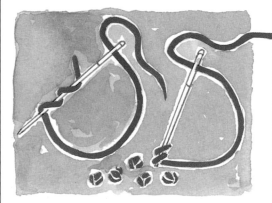

French knots. Bring the floss out of the canvas. Encircle the floss twice with the needle. Holding the floss firmly with the thumb twist the needle back into the canvas, close to where it first emerged.

RIBBON RINGS

Finished size: approximately 6 inches

Brightly colored narrow ribbons are used to create napkin rings, being worked in Scotch stitch over a 7-gauge plastic canvas which provides a firm background.

YOU WILL NEED
(for four rings)

- 14 x 6 inch piece of plastic canvas with 7 holes to 1 inch
- fine felt-tip pen with permanent ink
- 11 yards of ⅛ inch wide Offray Minidot ribbon in emerald
- 11 yards of ⅛ inch wide Offray Minidot ribbon in bright yellow
- tapestry needle, size 16
- 6 x 3 inch piece of felt in green and yellow
- fabric adhesive

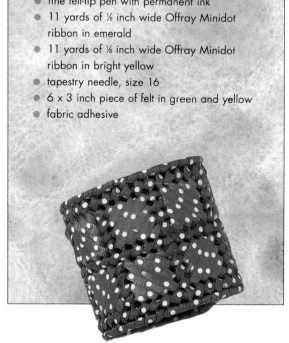

1 **To work** Each chart shows the complete design for one napkin ring. Each background square on the chart represents one hole of canvas. The design is worked throughout in Scotch stitch, but with the central straight stitches worked in opposite directions.

2 Following the chart, count out the number of holes for each ring. Use the felt-tip pen to mark out the outlines for the four rings, leaving at least two empty holes between each ring.

3 Work two rings using the green ribbon for the tent stitch (see page 18) and the yellow ribbon for the center slanted satin stitches; then work two rings in the reverse. Work each piece, following the chart and leaving the outer row of tent stitch unworked on each side edge.

4 When the needlepoint is complete, cut out each ring, leaving a margin of one unworked canvas thread all around each piece.

5 Make up each ring in the same way. Fold the canvas into a ring. Work tent stitch over the two edges to join them; fasten off the ribbon securely. Then overcast around the top and bottom of the ring in either yellow or green ribbon, being careful to cover the edges of the canvas.

6 For each ring, cut a piece of felt 6 x 1½ inches. Using fabric adhesive, glue the felt centrally over the inside of each ring, butting edges together to neaten.

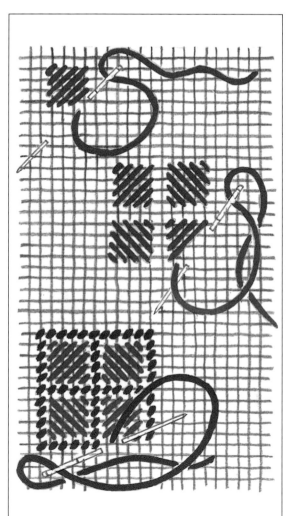

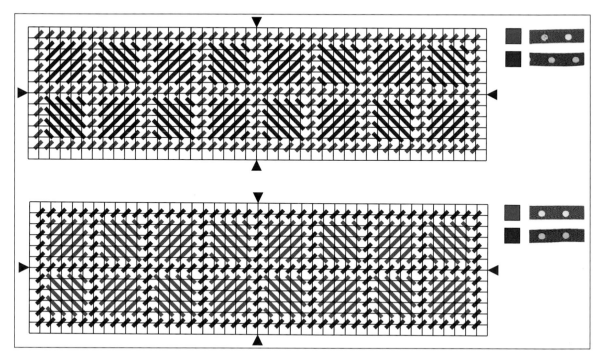

Scotch stitch. Work the slanted center stitches first, working over one, two, three, four, three, two, and one canvas thread. Work the next square of stitches in the opposite direction. Repeat, alternating the direction of the stitches. When the satin stitches are complete, outline the squares in tent stitch.

PUT YOUR FEET UP!

Finished size: to fit a footstool pad 14 x 12 inches

Variegated yarn is used to great effect on this stool top cover – the design includes just three shades of yarn, but their changing hues provide a richness and variety of tone. The footstool cover is worked in straight Gobelin stitch over a 12-gauge canvas.

YOU WILL NEED

- masking tape
- 21 x 19 inch piece of white mono interlock canvas with 12 holes to 1 inch
- needlepoint frame
- basting thread in contrasting color
- tapestry needle, size 18
- eight skeins of Brethyn Brith yarn in water
- six skeins of Brethyn Brith yarn in spring
- 12 skeins of Appletons yarn in mid blue 156
- footstool base with padded top 14 x 12 inches

1 To work To protect your hands and clothes, and prevent the yarn from catching on the canvas, fold masking tape evenly in half over the raw canvas edges.

2 Baste across the canvas both lengthwise and widthwise to mark the center.

3 Mount the canvas into the frame (see Techniques, page 10).

4 The chart shows just over one-quarter of the design. The center is marked with black arrowheads – match these up with the basting stitches on the canvas.

5 The design mirror-images vertically and horizontally along the center lines.

6 The design is worked in straight Gobelin stitch over four canvas threads, with a straight stitch to miter the blocks of stitches where they form a corner. Straight Gobelin stitch worked over two canvas threads is used to fill in, where necessary, around the edges.

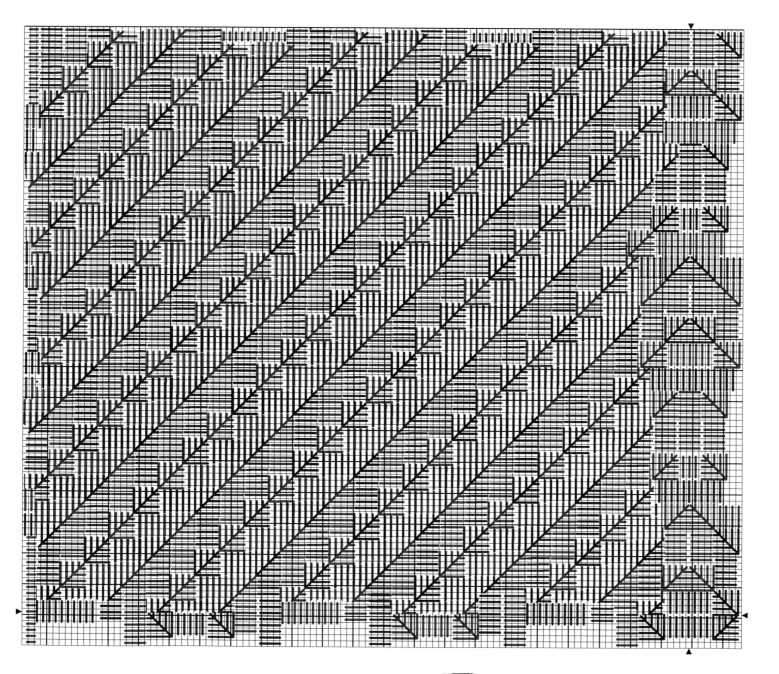

Mid Blue 156

Spring

Water

7 Work the first row out from the center, counting carefully. When this row is worked correctly, the whole pattern is set, and each row can be worked alongside the previous one. Work the rows, alternating the three yarn colors.

8 When the section shown is complete, work the remaining quarters in the same way.

9 **To finish** Remove the completed needlepoint from the frame. Peel off the masking tape and press on the wrong side over a damp cloth, gently pulling the canvas back into shape.

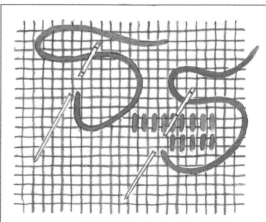

Straight Gobelin stitch. Bring the needle out of the canvas and insert four threads above. Bring the needle out to the left, ready for the second stitch. You can also work this stitch over two canvas threads to cover a smaller area.

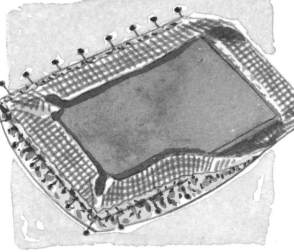

11 Turn the pad over and, using a staple gun, staple the canvas firmly in place to the underside of the pad. Remove tacks and replace pad into the stool base.

10 Remove the footstool pad from the base. Place the needlepoint centrally over the pad, and fold the surplus canvas to the back. Secure along the top edge with thumbtacks pushed into the pad. Pull the canvas taut over the opposite edge and secure with tacks in the same way. Repeat at both side edges.

PICTURE IT

Finished size: 7¾ x 6⅛ inches

For a stunning photo or picture frame, work textured stitches in tapestry yarn over a 10-gauge plastic canvas in this geometric design.

YOU WILL NEED

- two 7 x 8¾ inch pieces of plastic canvas with 10 holes to 1 inch plus two 1½ x 4¼ inch strips of canvas for the hinge
- DMC tapestry yarn in the following colors and amounts: 10 skeins of dark blue 7247, one skein each of pale blue 7798, sea green 7952, pine green 7906, purple 7242, and fuchsia pink 7155
- needlepoint frame
- tapestry needle, size 18
- black, fine-point felt-tip pen with permanent ink
- thin cardboard
- masking tape

1 **To work** For the frame front, mark the center of one piece of plastic canvas both lengthwise and widthwise. The chart shows the complete design of the frame front. The center of the design is marked with black arrowheads – match these up with the marked center lines on the canvas.

2 Work the design from the chart centrally over the canvas, placing the colors and stitches as shown in the key, but omitting the two single green borders.

3 When the needlepoint is complete, cut out the front, leaving a margin of one unworked canvas thread all around the outer and inner (aperture) edge of the embroidery.

4 Work a row of overcast stitch around the inner (aperture) edge of the frame in pine green 7906.

5 Lay the front over the second piece of canvas, matching the canvas holes. Carefully draw around the outer edge of the front with felt-tip pen, to mark the outline of the frame back on the second piece of canvas. Cut a horizontal slit in the center of the drawn rectangle on the back, making the slit 1⅜ inch across and approximately ⅛ inch deep.

6 Fill in the areas inside the drawn rectangle with reversed mosaic stitch (see page 30) worked in dark blue 7247, leaving a margin of one unworked canvas thread inside the edge of the rectangle and around the slit. Check that the worked area is exactly the same size and covers the same number of threads as the front. Now cut out the back, taking care to leave a margin of one unworked canvas thread around the edge.

7 Cover both strips of canvas with reversed mosaic stitch in dark blue 7247, to match the back. Leave one thread unworked around the outer edge.

8 To make the hinge, cut a strip of cardboard 1¼ x 3½ inches. Sandwich the cardboard strip between the two pieces of worked needlepoint, wrong sides together. Push the cardboard down to one end. Overcast the two pieces together using dark blue 7247.

■	**7247 RM**
■	**7798 DL**
■	**7952 DL**
■	**7906 WC**
■	**7242 RM**
■	**7155 C**

RM: Reversed Mosaic

DL: Double Leviathan

WC: Woven Cross

C: Chequer

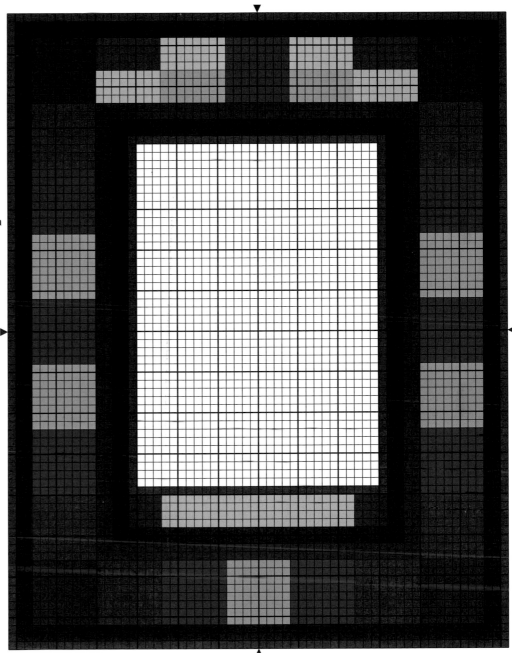

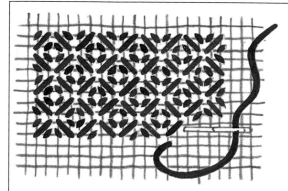

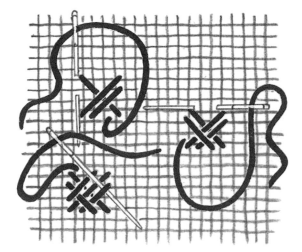

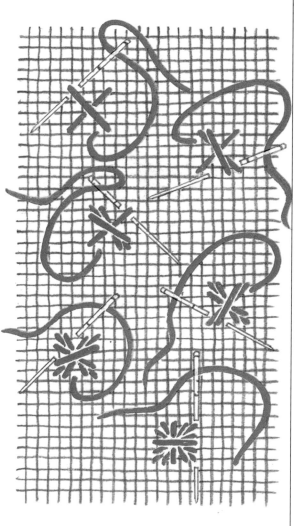

Reversed Mosaic stitch. Each block of this stitch is made up of a diagonal stitch worked over two vertical and two horizontal canvas threads at the center of two short diagonal stitches. Work each block individually, changing the slant of the stitches on alternate blocks.

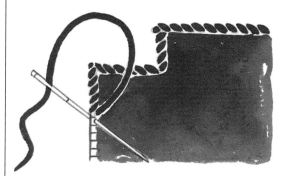

Woven Cross stitch. Work the blocks in horizontal rows. Begin with a large, standard cross stitch over four vertical and four horizontal canvas threads. Overstitch the cross with four diagonal straight stitches, which should be woven over and under each other as they are stitched. Place each row of stitches directly above the previous row.

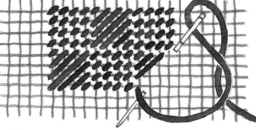

Overcast stitch. This stitch is used to finish or join two pieces of plastic canvas. Work either from right to left, or from left to right. Work diagonal stitches over the canvas edge. Take one stitch in each hole along a straight edge, but take two or three stitches in a hole on an inside or outside corner to make sure that you cover the canvas edge.

Checker stitch. Work blocks of stitches over four vertical and four horizontal canvas threads. Alternate blocks of 16 tent stitches with blocks of diagonal stitches, making sure that all the stitches slant in the same direction.

Double Leviathan stitch. Start by working a large cross stitch over four vertical and four horizontal canvas threads. Then work a series of crossing stitches over the top, following the order shown here.

9 **Making up the frame** Push the end of the hinge without the cardboard through the slit in the back panel, until about ¼ inch protrudes on the wrong side. Secure the hinge firmly in place with several stitches.

10 Cut a 5⅞ x 7¼ inch piece of cardboard. Lay the front embroidery over the cardboard and mark the position of the aperture with a pencil. Center the photograph or picture, right side up, over the pencil lines, and secure with strips of masking tape.

11 Place the front and back together, with wrong sides facing, and slip the cardboard in between. Overcast the front and back together with pine green 7906, taking care to fasten off the thread ends neatly.

BOX CLEVER

Finished size: to fit a trinket box with a 3-inch lid

Keep all your trinkets and treasures in this pretty box, decorated with a tiny beaded pansy. Worked over a 14-gauge canvas, each stitch holds a bead offset by a stitched background of varigated embroidery floss.

YOU WILL NEED

- 7 inch square of mono interlock canvas with 14 holes to 1 inch
- masking tape
- one packet of glass seed beads in the following colors: dark purple, mauve, crimson, dark red, and yellow
- Anchor embroidery floss in the following colors and amounts: one skein each of dark purple 102, mauve 100, dark red 45, crimson 59, yellow 291, variegated deep pink 1204
- circular wooden trinket box with 3 inch diameter lid
- tapestry needle, size 20
- crewel needle, size 10
- fine-point, black felt-tip pen with permanent ink
- needlepoint frame

1 **To work** To protect your hands and clothes, and the canvas from unraveling, fold the masking tape evenly in half over the raw canvas edges.

2 Trace the actual-size pansy onto a clean sheet of paper. Go over the outline with black felt-tip pen.

3 Tape the paper flat, then tape the canvas centrally over the design. Draw the design onto the canvas using the felt-tip pen.

4 Mount the canvas into the frame (see Techniques, page 10).

5 Work the pansy, following the actual-size motif and key. Work the beaded areas in tent stitch using two strands of embroidery floss in the crewel needle. Attach one bead with each stitch.

6 Stitch all the background in half cross stitch, using six strands of embroidery floss in the needle. Work the background up to the circular outline.

7 When the needlepoint is complete, carefully cut it out around the circular outline and fit inside the box lid, following the manufacturer's instructions.

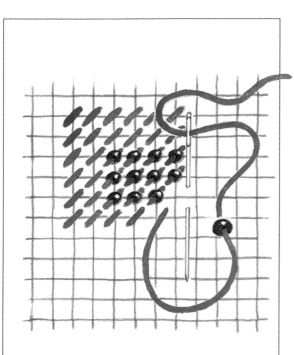

■	102
■	100
■	45
■	59
■	291
□	1204

Half-cross stitch. Bring the needle out of the canvas and take a small diagonal stitch over one canvas thread intersection with the needle vertical, bringing it out of the canvas directly below. On the wrong side of the canvas the stitches will be vertical. Make sure that all the stitches slant in the same direction. When working with beads, bring the needle out of the canvas, pick up one bead and take the needle back down into the canvas. The beads will slant in the opposite direction to the stitches.

BE MINE

Finished size: approximately 14 inch square

This unusual pillow is worked in a variety of stitches over a 10-gauge canvas. Each square is worked in a different stitch and outlined in tent stitch, and tassels at each corner of the pillow are the perfect finish.

YOU WILL NEED

- 18 inch square of white mono canvas with 10 threads to 1 inch
- masking tape
- basting thread in contrasting color
- tapestry needle, size 18
- needlepoint frame
- DMC tapestry yarns in the following colors and amounts: seven skeins of blue 7318, five skeins each of pink 7804 and blue 7319, four skeins each of blue 7314 and white, three skeins of pink 7708, two skeins of pink 7600, and one skein of yellow 7726
- 16 inch square of fabric for backing
- matching sewing thread
- 12 inch zipper
- 14 inch square pillow form
- 1¾ yard of cord
- four tassels, or four skeins of DMC tapestry yarn in blue 7318

1 To work To protect your hands and clothes, and the yarn from catching on the canvas edges, fold masking tape evenly in half over the raw canvas edges.

2 Baste lengthwise and widthwise across the canvas, using a contrasting sewing thread, to mark the center (see Techniques, page 10).

3 The chart shows the complete design for the pillow. The center is marked by black arrowheads, which must match up with the basting stitches on the canvas. Each background square on the chart represents one hole of canvas.

4 From the center, count out the holes and mark the squares that make up the design.

5 Fit the canvas into the frame (see Techniques, page 10).

6 The design is worked in a variety of needlepoint stitches. Work the design, following the chart for the stitches and the key for the yarn colors. Begin by working the central heart and square in velvet and diagonal mosaic stitch, then outline each of the remaining squares with a row of tent stitches (see page 18).

7 Fill in each square with the appropriate needlepoint stitch. In some cases, the stitches on the outside of each square will have to be shortened to fill the area.

8 When the design is complete, remove the canvas from the frame. Peel off the masking tape. Press gently on the wrong side over a damp cloth, gently pulling the canvas back into shape (see Techniques, page 13).

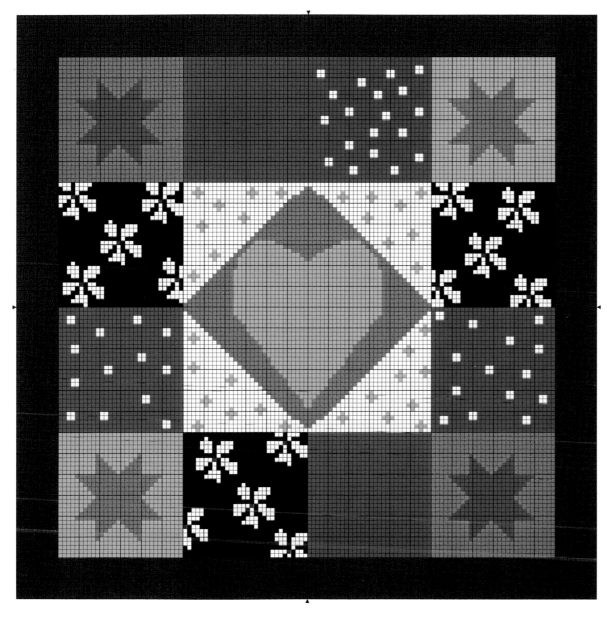

| white | 7314 | 7318 | 7319 | 7600 | 7708 | 7726 | 7804 |

rice	byzantine	slanted gobelin	rice
cross		velvet	cross
slanted gobelin	hungarian	diagonal mosaic	slanted gobelin
rice	cross	cashmere	rice

9 For the back, cut two pieces of fabric, 15 x 8¼ inches. Place right sides together, and pin and baste across the center. Stitch in from each side, leaving a 12 inch central opening; press seam open.

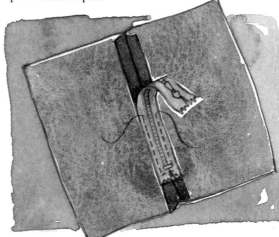

10 Place zipper, face down, over the basted seam; pin and baste. Turn fabric over and, with a zipper foot on the machine, stitch around zipper; partially open zipper.

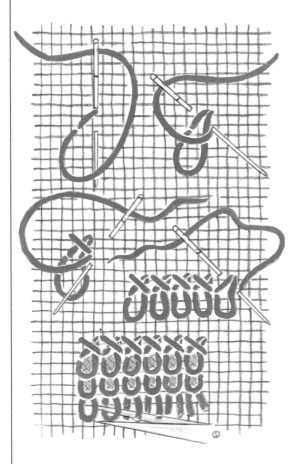

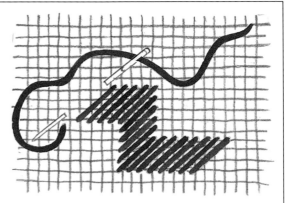

11 Place back and front right sides together; pin and stitch all around. Trim, and turn right side out through zipper. Insert pillow form and close zipper.

12 Handsew cord around outer edge, slotting ends neatly into seam. Add tassels. To make tassels, cut two short lengths of yarn; tie one around a skein 1¼ inch from top. Slot second length through top loop and tie. Remove skein bands. Trim tassel to 5½ inches.

Velvet stitch. This stitch is worked upward from left to right. Bring the needle out of the canvas, and insert two threads up and two threads to the right. Bring the needle out again at the first hole and hold down a loop of yarn while taking a vertical stitch. Take the final stitch over the canvas, forming a cross with the first stitch. When the rows are complete, cut and trim the loops.

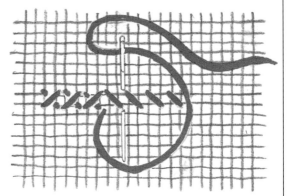

Byzantine stitch. Work satin stitches diagonally over four vertical and four horizontal canvas threads. This creates a woven, step effect.

Cross stitch. Bring the needle out of the canvas and take a stitch two threads to the left and two threads up to form the half cross. Complete the crosses working in the opposite direction.

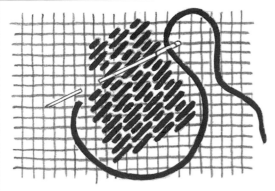

Cashmere stitch. Work diagonal stitches in sequence over one, two, and two canvas intersections, with the lower end of each stitch falling exactly beneath the other and with each set of three stitches moving one thread to the right each time when working diagonally downward. When working upward from right to left, move the three stitches one thread to the left.

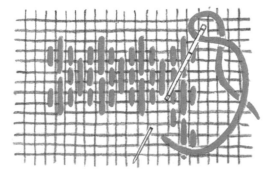

Hungarian stitch. This stitch can be worked in one or two different colors. Take vertical straight stitches over two, four, and two horizontal threads of canvas, leaving two vertical threads between each group of stitches. Fit each row alternately into the preceding row.

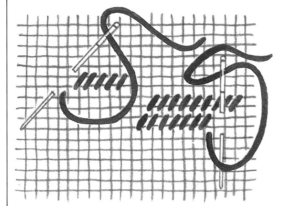

Slanted Gobelin. This stitch can be worked from right to left, or from left to right. Work each stitch over two horizontal and one vertical canvas threads.

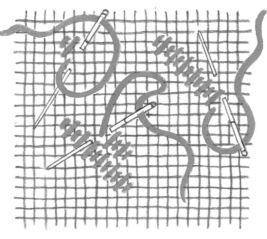

Diagonal Mosaic stitch. Work down the canvas from left to right, and then up again. Work over one, two, and one canvas thread. Fit the next row so the short stitches are next to the long stitches.

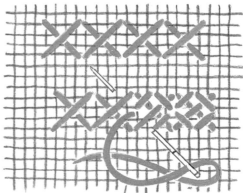

Rice stitch. First cover the area with cross stitch, worked over four canvas threads. Then work a small diagonal stitch over each corner of the cross stitch over two canvas threads.

MAGIC CARPET

Finished size: 39½ x 28 inches

*T*urn fabric strips into a woven carpet by working Parisian stitch over a rug canvas. The alternating rows of two cotton fabrics will create an attractive, hardwearing rug.

YOU WILL NEED

- 4½ yards of 45 inch wide cotton fabric, such as Madras, in two different designs
- rotary cutter
- 46 x 28 inch piece of rug canvas with 3½ holes to 1 inch
- bodkin needle
- 3¾ yards of ¼ inch piping cord

1 **To work** To prepare the fabric strips, cut out 1¾ inch wide strips from across the fabric.

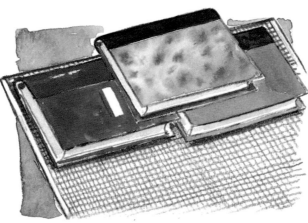

2 Lay the canvas on the table with the selvages on either side. Place a heavy object on the canvas end to prevent it slipping.

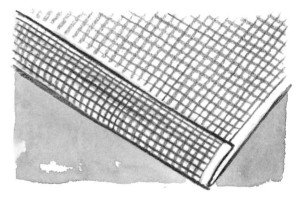

3 Count up the first eight rows; fold the canvas along the eighth row to the right side. Leaving two holes free, work the first few rows through both thicknesses of canvas.

4 Work each row in Parisian stitch, but take the long stitches over eight threads and the short stitches over four threads of canvas. Alternate the two fabrics, row by row.

5 Neaten all the fabric ends by running them through a few stitches on the wrong side when beginning a new length or ending a length of fabric.

6 Work across the canvas until you reach the last 16 rows, then turn the canvas up and work the final rows through double canvas, in the same way as before.

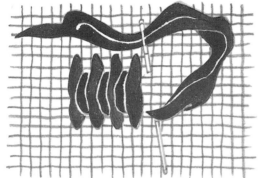

Parisian stitch. Working from left to right, bring the fabric through the canvas and insert the needle eight threads above, bringing the needle out six threads down and one thread to the right. To make the short stitches, insert the needle four threads up and come out six threads down and one thread to the right, ready for the next long stitch.

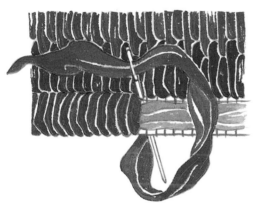

7 To neaten the edge, fold piping cord inside a fabric strip and lay along outer edge of rug. Overcast over the piping, turning under raw edge of strip and overlapping the stitches.

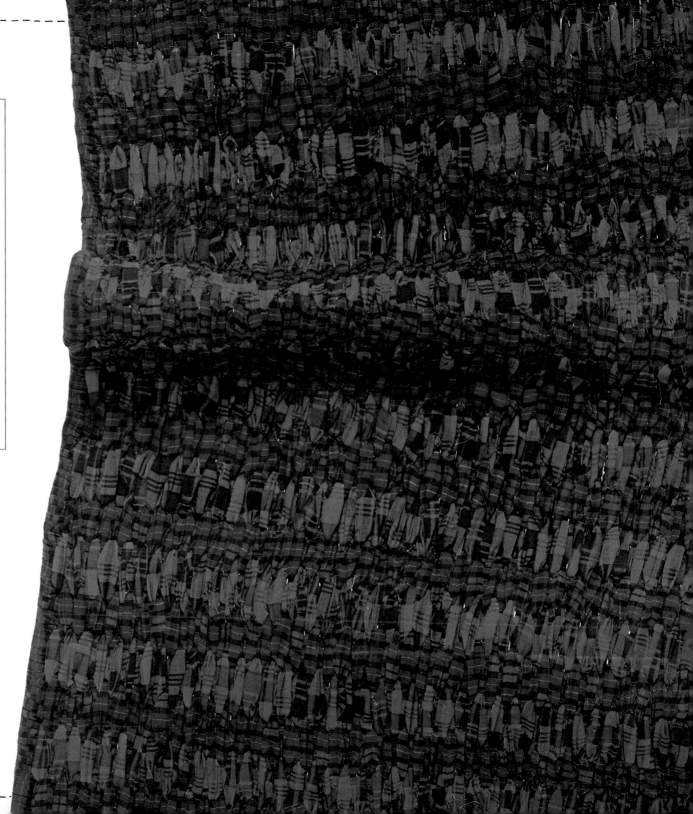

FLORENTINE NEEDLECASE

Finished size: 4¾ x 3½ inches

Worked in traditional Florentine stitch, this pretty needlecase will be a bonus for any sewing kit. Use stranded yarn and work over a 12-gauge canvas, then add felt leaves and complete with a twisted yarn edge.

YOU WILL NEED

- 10 x 8½ inch piece of mono canvas with 12 holes to 1 inch
- masking tape
- basting thread in contrasting color
- tapestry needle, size 18
- needlepoint frame
- Paternayan Persian yarn in the following colors and amounts: one skein each of dark pink 350, medium pink 353, pale pink 354, and yellow 772
- 8 x 6 inch piece of cotton fabric for lining
- sewing thread to match lining fabric
- 5½ x 4¾ inch piece of pink felt
- 5 x 4¼ inch piece of yellow felt
- pinking shears

1 **To work** To protect your hands and clothes, and the yarn from catching on the canvas edges, fold masking tape evenly in half over the raw canvas edges.

2 Baste both lengthwise and widthwise across the canvas, using a contrasting sewing thread, to mark the center (see Techniques, Page 10). Now mark the outline of the needlecase, 6½ x 4¾ inches, on to the canvas.

3 Mount the canvas into the frame (see Techniques, page 10).

4 The chart shows the rows of Florentine stitch that are worked in rows across the needlecase. The center is marked with black arrowheads, which must match the basting stitches on the canvas. Each background square on the chart represents one hole of canvas. Repeat the rows, working the colors in order.

5 Work the first row across the center of the canvas using dark pink 350 to set the pattern, working each stitch over four canvas threads. Then work each row in the same way above and below the first row, working the rows in color order, until the whole area is filled. At the side edges, some stitches will have to be shortened to fill the gaps.

6 When the needlepoint is complete, remove it from the frame. Peel off the masking tape and press lightly on the wrong side over a damp cloth, gently pulling the canvas back into shape.

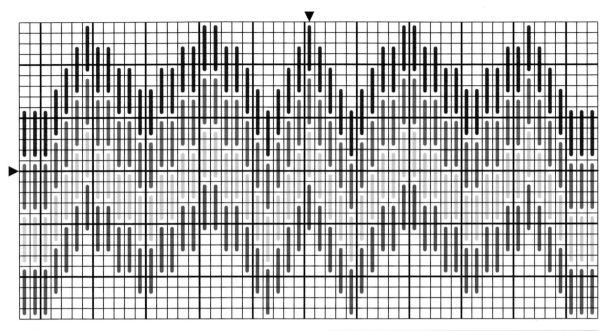

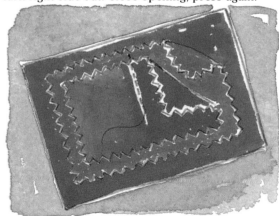

■	350
■	353
■	354
■	772

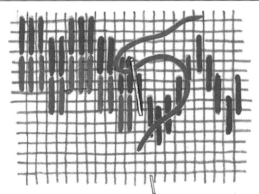

Florentine stitch. This stitch is used for working Florentine patterns, with two or more colors forming a wave design. The size of the wave will vary, depending upon the number of stitches or the number of threads over which the stitches are worked.

7 Place the canvas onto the lining with right sides facing; pin and stitch against the stitched area all around, leaving an opening in one side. Trim off corners and across seams, and turn right side out. Close opening; press again.

8 Using pinking shears, trim the two pieces of felt for the inner leaves. Lay the leaves centrally, one on top of the other, and position centrally onto the lining side of the needlecase. Handsew the leaves in place by stitching down the center.

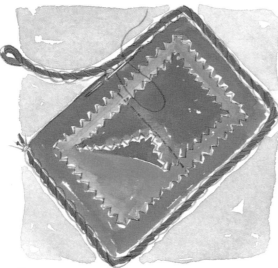

9 Measure around the outer edge of
needlecase. Cut six strands each of pink 350
and yellow 772 to three times this length. Tie
ends together. Slot one end over a door handle.
Slide a pencil into opposite loop. Keep turning
the pencil to twist the yarn. When tightly
twisted, remove from handle and hold ends
together while yarn twists together to form a
cord. Handsew around case, neatening the ends.

FABULOUS FLORALS

Finished size: approximately 28½ x 4¾ inches

YOU WILL NEED
(for one pair of tiebacks)

- 20 x 40 inch piece of white mono interlock canvas with 12 holes to 1 inch
- masking tape
- basting thread in contrasting color
- tapestry needle, size 20
- DMC tapestry yarn in the following colors: 22 skeins of ecru, four skeins each of dusky pink 7204, dark dusky pink 7205, pale rose 7132, medium rose 7760, dark rose 7759, pale green 7369, gray/green 7394, olive green 7396, dark olive green 7398, three skeins each of crimson 7212, deep rose 7758, yellow ochre 7504, two skeins each of mid crimson 7210, sea green 7326, dark sea green 7327, yellow/brown 7505, brown 7508, mauve 7896, deep purple 7228, one skein of gray/blue 7323, and deep mauve 7255
- needlepoint frame
- 32 x 16 inch piece of cotton fabric for lining
- 30 x 11 inch piece of interfacing
- 4½ yards of corded piping
- sewing thread to match lining fabric
- four ½ inch diameter curtain rings

Hold back your curtains in style with this pretty flower-strewn tieback. Worked in tapestry yarn over a 12-gauge canvas, this beautiful addition to your home furnishings will last a lifetime.

1 **To work** To protect your hands and clothes, and the yarn from catching on the edge, fold masking tape evenly in half over the raw canvas edges.

2 Baste both lengthwise and widthwise across the canvas, using a contrasting thread, to mark the center (see Techniques, page 10). Both tiebacks can be worked one above the other, with a gap of about 2¾ inches between them.

3 Mount the canvas into the frame (see Techniques, page 10).

4 The chart shows the right-hand side of one tieback with the center marked by black arrowheads, which must match up with the basting threads on the canvas. Each background square on the chart represents one tent stitch worked over one intersection of canvas. To complete the left-hand side of the tieback, reverse the section shown, and work from the center outward.

5 Work the design throughout in tent stitch, following the chart and key for colors. Begin by stitching the flowers, leaves, and other motifs across the whole tieback, then fill in the background in ecru.

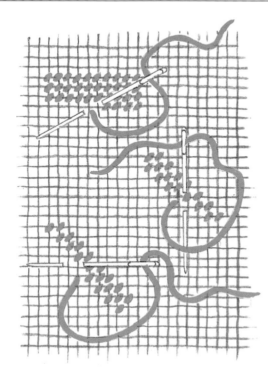

Tent stitch. To work horizontal rows, bring the needle out of the canvas and take a small diagonal stitch over one canvas thread intersection. Take the needle down diagonally behind one horizontal and two vertical threads, then bring it out ready for the next stitch. On the wrong side, the stitches will be slightly longer diagonal stitches.

To work diagonally down the canvas, take the needle diagonally up over one canvas thread intersection then pass it vertically down behind two horizontal canvas threads.

To work diagonally up the canvas, the stitches are worked in the same way but the needle is passed horizontally behind two vertical threads.

6 When the needlepoint is complete, remove it from the frame. Peel off the masking tape and press on the wrong side over a damp cloth, gently pulling the canvas back into shape.

7 Cut out each needlepoint piece, leaving a ⅜ inch border all around. Use the needlepoint as a pattern to cut one piece from the lining and one piece from the interfacing to the same size.

8 Place the interfacing onto the wrong side of needlepoint, catchstitching together around the outside edge. Pin the piping around needlepoint, on the right side, with the piping facing inward and edges matching. Join ends together to fit.

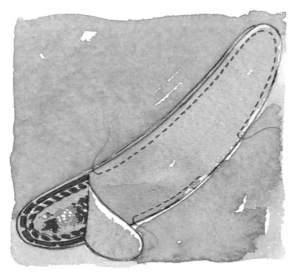

9 Place lining fabric on to the needlepoint with right sides facing; pin and stitch against the needlepoint all round, leaving an opening in one side. Trim and turn right side out. Turn in opening edges and slipstitch to close.

10 Handsew a curtain ring to both ends of the tieback.

■ 7212	■ 7759	■ 7369	■ 7505
■ 7210	■ 7758	■ 7228	■ 7508
■ 7205	■ 7398	■ 7255	■ 7323
■ 7204	■ 7396	■ 7896	■ 7326
■ 7132	■ 7394	■ 7504	■ 7327
■ 7760			

BELT AND BUTTONS

Finished size: Belt: 25 x 1½ inches Buttons: 1¼ inch diameter

Stitch a matching pair of stylish self-covered buttons and belt for a child. Worked in pearl cotton in cross-cornered cushion stitch, choose colors to suit the outfit.

YOU WILL NEED

- belt: 29 x 5½ inch piece of white mono interlock canvas with 14 holes to 1 inch
- buttons: 8½ inch square of white mono interlock canvas with 14 holes to 1 inch
- masking tape
- DMC pearl cotton no 5 in the following colors and amounts: two skeins of navy 939, one skein each of green 502, orange 742, mauve 208, red 321, pink 893, and blue 792
- tapestry needle, size 20
- needlepoint frame
- 26 x 2¾ inch piece of navy blue cotton fabric
- 25 x 1½ inch piece of medium-weight fusible interfacing
- basting thread
- three hook and eye fasteners
- Self-covering buttons, 1¼ inch in diameter

1 **To work the belt** To prevent the canvas edges from unraveling, and to protect your hands and clothes, fold masking tape evenly in half over the raw canvas edges.

2 Mount the canvas into the frame (see Techniques, page 10).

3 The chart shows a section of the design, which is repeated across the canvas. Each square on the chart represents one hole of canvas.

4 Beginning 2 inches in from one short edge, work an outline of tent stitch (see page 18) centrally across the canvas in navy 939, following the chart.

5 Fill in the spaces with cross-cornered cushion stitch, using the remaining six colored embroidery threads randomly.

6 To complete the belt, work a row of plaited stitch all around the outer edge in navy 939.

7 **To finish** Remove the completed needlepoint from the frame. Peel off the masking tape from the canvas edges. Press the needlepoint on the wrong side over a damp cloth, gently pulling the canvas back into shape.

8 Turn in all edges along the line of the needlepoint, and press. Trim raw canvas edges, as necessary.

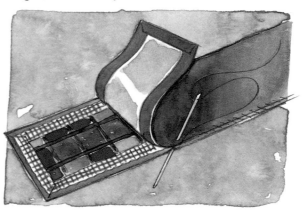

9 Fuse the interfacing centrally to wrong side of fabric strip. Turn in raw edges of fabric strip for ⅜ inch. Place strip to needlepoint belt with wrong sides facing. Slipstitch the fabric to the needlepoint all around the outer edge.

10 Handsew three hooks and eyes to short edges, so belt edges butt neatly together.

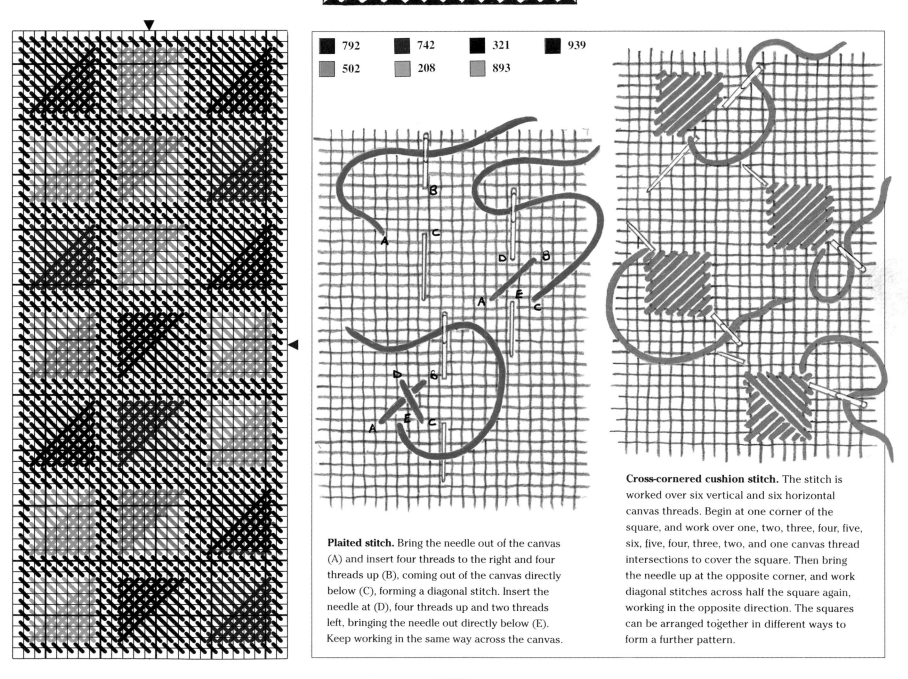

	792		742		321		939
	502		208		893		

Plaited stitch. Bring the needle out of the canvas (A) and insert four threads to the right and four threads up (B), coming out of the canvas directly below (C), forming a diagonal stitch. Insert the needle at (D), four threads up and two threads left, bringing the needle out directly below (E). Keep working in the same way across the canvas.

Cross-cornered cushion stitch. The stitch is worked over six vertical and six horizontal canvas threads. Begin at one corner of the square, and work over one, two, three, four, five, six, five, four, three, two, and one canvas thread intersections to cover the square. Then bring the needle up at the opposite corner, and work diagonal stitches across half the square again, working in the opposite direction. The squares can be arranged together in different ways to form a further pattern.

11 **Buttons** Divide the canvas equally into four with contrasting thread. Work one four-square pattern in the center of each canvas section, working with random colors, in the same way as for the belt.

12 Cut out and fit the canvas into a button mold, following the manufacturers' instructions.